The Springfield Carbine on the Western Frontier
– Revised –

KENNETH M. HAMMER

PREFACE

This book has been prepared as a sketch for studying the trapdoor carbine used by the cavalry in the Indian Wars period. My appreciation is extended to the many who contributed to its preparation, particularly to Stephen W. Rose of Casper, Wyoming for his expert knowledge of cartridges of the Indian Wars period; to James S. Hutchins, emeritus historian, National Museum of American History, and to Lieut. Col. Vern Smalley of Bozeman, Montana for their helpful comments. Vern also served as editor, researcher, typist and publisher.

Muskego, Wisconsin   Kenneth Hammer

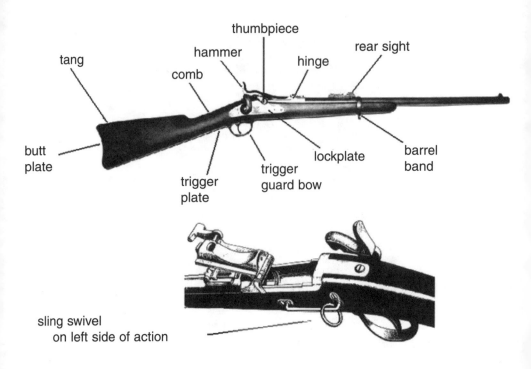
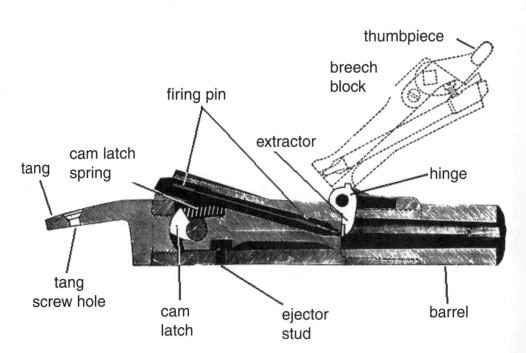

Vertical section of the Allin breach-loading system

THE SPRINGFIELD CARBINE ON THE WESTERN FRONTIER

A commonly-used weapon among the dragoons and cavalry was the Model 1852 Sharp's .52-caliber percussion carbine which began to reach the field in 1858 and 1859 to replace the Model 1847 musketoon carbine. In 1858 the commander at Fort Buchanan in today's southern Arizona asked for the Sharps for his garrison, citing the superior characteristics. He wrote: *". . . Dragoon soldiers have more confidence in it than any other weapon I have seen put in their hands."* It became a favorite of the regular cavalry, and California volunteers carried this model through the Civil War. The Model 1863 Sharps was an improvement over the Model 1859 and was widely used by cavalry companies until the Model 1873 Springfield carbine replaced it.

The Model 1873 Springfield carbine, the "trapdoor carbine" of the Indian Wars period, became the standard issue for the U.S. Army's cavalry. Its use standardized shoulder arms, for near the end of the Civil War there were some 65 different shoulder weapons used by the federal army. The Union cavalry had used various breech-loaders, including Sharps and Spencer carbines of different calibers, bullet weights, and powder charges. To eliminate the confusing types and calibers it was necessary to standardize on some type of breech-loader. In the latter part of the war, Brig. Gen. Alexander B. Dyer, Chief of Ordnance, directed Erskine S. Allin, Master Armorer at the National Armory at Springfield, Massachusetts, to develop a breech mechanism that would allow economical conversion of Civil War muzzle-loading, percussion weapons to breech-loaders using self-contained metallic cartridges. Dyer directed Allin to use any existing ideas regardless of patents.

Allin patented a single-shot, breech-loading system on September 19, 1865 under U.S. Patent No.49959. Using this patent, the National Armory converted a small number of .58-caliber muzzle-loading arms, the Model 1865, for use in the post-Civil War period. The government paid claims of $124,341 to various inventors holding patents infringed by features of the Allin breech-loader.

A Board of Officers appointed by the Secretary of War in March 1865, recommended reducing .58-caliber weapons to .50 caliber to save on the amount of lead required for bullets and to reduce the weight for the soldier. The Allin breech-loading system was used in the production of the U.S. Carbine, Model 1866.

Following the recommendation of the 1865 Board, surplus barrels of .58 caliber were reamed to accept .50-caliber liners which were brazed in place. Subsequently-produced U.S. Carbines, Model 1868, were largely made with steel barrels, rather than re-lined barrels. Only a small number of these carbines were made, essentially for field trials.

Experiments were also conducted at Frankford Arsenal, near Philadelphia, to perfect a practical center-fire cartridge for service weapons. The Martin bar-anvil-primed cartridge was the first inside-primed cartridge to be produced in quantity for use in Springfield arms. Manufacture of this .50-70-450 cartridge was begun in October 1866 at Frankford Arsenal. The cartridge was so designated since it was of .50 caliber (.50-inch inside barrel diameter), contained 70 grains of powder and had a 450-grain bullet. Production ended in March 1868. Remaining stores of this cartridge were used for some time afterwards, as empty cases have been found on western military sites established years after this date.

The second inside-primed cartridge used the Benet-cup primer in place of the Martin bar-anvil. In March 1868, production of .50-70-450 cartridges, using the Benet-cup primer, began at Frankford Arsenal for use in the Model 1868 carbines and rifles (the latter being a longer-barrel version of the carbines). With variations in size and material, the Benet-cup primer remained in use from 1868 to 1882.

Production of the .50-70-450 Benet-primed cartridge ended in December, 1873. Remaining supplies were used long after 1873. This cartridge was occasionally produced as late as 1882 and intended for the militia rather than the regular army. Both the Martin-bar-primed and the Benet-primed cartridges had non-reloadable copper-alloy cases with the primer anvils secured in the case by crimping.

From 1868 to 1873 (and occasionally after) large lots of .50-70-450 ammunition were produced on federal contract by Winchester Repeating Arms Co., the United States Cartridge Co., and the Union Metallic Cartridge Co. This ammunition was usually brass-cased and had Berdan, Boxer or Farrington primers.

Early in 1870 a Board of Officers, headed by Brig. Gen. John M. Schofield, met in St. Louis to test new weapons for the army. About 50 different weapons were submitted for test. After a series of tests the Board recommended adoption of the Remington Rolling Block model. However, in view of the preference of company commanders, the Allin system was continued. Thus followed the Model 1870 carbine of which 1,828 were issued. The Model 1870 was similar to the Model 1868, except for changes in the barrel, breech-block, receiver and sights.

The Model 1870 had a round barrel, 21.75 inches long, rifled with three broad grooves having one turn in 42 inches. The overall length was 41.375 inches and the weight was about 7.94 pounds. An oval barrel was fitted to the oiled black-walnut stock, the latter being 29.87 inches long. The curved butt was fitted with a steel plate marked "US" on the tang. A sliding ring on a swivel bar on the left side of the stock was used for hooking the carbine to the cavalryman's carbine sling, which was slung over his head and left shoulder. The front sight was on a stud base and a folding, slide leaf, rear sight was used. The beveled lockplate was inletted into the stock and was stamped with the spread eagle and "US Springfield" in two lines forward of the hammer. There was a date behind the hammer which was usually "1865" as Civil War lockplates were used in assembly. The breech-block was stamped "Model 1870" and metal parts were finished bright on most carbines. Some were blued or browned and had case-hardened colors on the lockplate.

The cavalry regiments received 259 Model 1870 carbines in 1871 for field trials, in addition to 150 Remington half-stock and 94 Remington full-stock and 1,256 Sharps carbines. In 1872 there were 150 Ward-Burton, bolt-action carbines issued to the cavalry for field trials.

Company F, 7th Cavalry, was issued 21 each of the Remington full-stock, Sharps and Springfield carbines on June 13, 1871, and 21 Ward-Burton's on April 16, 1872. Lieut. Charles Larned of Company F had this to say about the weapons:

> "Whenever the arms were in the hands of the men, it was noticed that the piece (that) seemingly required the least attention in manipulation of loading was the Government Springfield carbine. A proper allowance, however, should be made in that respect in favor of the Ward-Burton and Remington, both of which, and particularly the former, are less familiar to them than the Springfield. For rapidity of fire there appears to be little choice between the Ward-Burton and the Springfield, both of which excell in that respect the Remington, as their facilities for ejecting cartridges are superior to those of the latter. This superiority appears to rise from the fact, first, of their greater leverage, by which a tight cartridge is withdrawn without difficulty, the same affecting its insertion; second that in the latter piece the thumb, in drawing back the breech-block, is generally in the way of the falling cartridge . . . . The mechanism of the former, although somewhat cumbersome, appears to be sufficiently strong, and to perform all its functions with the greatest efficiency . . . ."

Complaints against the Springfield were that the stock should be stronger, the rear sight should fall forward instead of to the rear and the breech-block was liable to open from jolting in the saddle. The cartridge failure rate was 1.96% for the 96,479 cartridges fired in field trials, the lowest rate for any of the field trial arms. The Springfield was preferred because of minimal misfires, breakage and extraction difficulties.

The army was not satisfied with the performance of the Model 1870 and the .50-caliber cartridge. An Ordnance Board convened in 1872 under Brig. Gen. Alfred Terry to select a breech-loading system for carbines and rifles. For eight months the Board examined about 108 different arms, some developed in Europe. After reviewing reports from the field, which were 12 to 1 in favor of the Springfield, the Board recommended on May 5, 1873, that the Springfield be retained in the service. An Ordnance Board headed by Col. James Benton, at the same time, recommended that the caliber of all shoulder and side arms be standardized at .45 caliber.

The National Armory manufactured the next model, the U.S. Carbine, Model

1873. This differed from the Model 1870 mainly in the reduction in caliber from .50 to .45. The pitch of the rifling (.005" depth) was increased to one turn in 22 inches. A thinner, unbeveled lockplate mounted flush with the stock, a rounded hammer and a strengthened ejector stud were used. A round steel barrel replaced the iron barrel of the Model 1870. The heads of a number of screws were rounded off and all metal parts were chemically blued to a dark blue. The rear sight was enlarged and moved forward, a stacking swivel was attached under the band and the breech-block was stamped "Model 1873." The overall length (for all standard models from 1873 to 1888) was 41.313 inches. The barrel length for all standard models was 21.875 inches. A plain butt with "US" stamped on the tang was fitted to the one-piece, walnut stock of 30 inches length. The weight was reduced to about 6.87 pounds.

The Allin breech-loading system consisted of a rising breech-block with a swing-up hinge at the forward end of the block. The front of the breech-block was hinged securely in position by two circular receiving rings and a strong hingepin. In closing, a cam-lock in the rear of the long breech-block rotated under a circular projection at the top rear of the receiver. The trigger pull was smooth but long. The hammer blow was long, heavy and slow. The cartridge was fired by a long pin seated in the breech-block and struck by a conventional side hammer. After the carbine had been fired, the camlock was released by unlatching the thumbpiece and the breech-block then swung up, ejecting the empty case and exposing the breech for reloading. The extractor and ejector readily cleared the action of the fired case. The well in the breech-block guided the next cartridge into the chamber. The breech-block and close-coupled hinge provided the shooter with considerable seating power for stubborn cases. The Model 1873 was superior to most carbines for use in sandy, dusty country as the breech block and receiver could easily be wiped.

The standard loading of the .45-caliber carbine cartridge was 55 grains of dense musket powder (a.k.a. black powder) while that for the rifle cartridge was 70 grains. The Benet-cup primer was continued as the standard ignition. Both the carbine and rifle used a 405-grain bullet (not 450 grain). Pasteboard *wads* or *liners* were used within the powder cavity in the carbine load to fill the space created by the smaller powder charge. The bullet was round-nosed and had three wide, deep cannelures filled with Bayberry tallow or Japan wax.

The hardened bullet consisted of 1 part tin to 16 parts lead. The case was the same for both carbine and rifle cartridges; it was 2.1 inches in length with a straight taper and was made of Bloomfield gilding metal (copper alloy). Total carbine cartridge weight was about 611 grains, packed 20 cartridges in a cardboard box. A box of 1,000 rounds weighed roughly 90 pounds and was packed as follows:

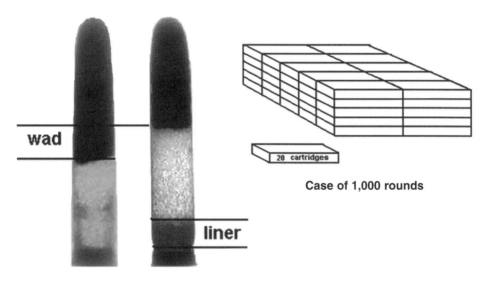

X-rays of .45-55 cartridges

Case of 1,000 rounds

Facsimile of Frankford Arsenal Ammunition Boxes

20
U. S. SPRINGFIELD CARBINE
CARTRIDGES,
CALIBRE, .45
Charge, 55 grains Musket Powder. Bullet, 405 grains
Frankford Arsenal,
JULY, 1874.

20
U. S. SPRINGFIELD RIFLE
CARTRIDGES,
CALIBRE, .45
Charge, 70 grains Musket Powder. Bullet, 405 grains
Frankford Arsenal,
AUG. 1874.

20
U. S. SPRINGFIELD RIFLE
CARTRIDGES,
CALIBRE, .45
Charge, 70 grains Musket Powder. Bullet, 405 grains
Frankford Arsenal,
APRIL, 1875

Production of Benet-primed .45-caliber carbine cartridges began in September, 1873, and continued to July 1882. Rifle cartridge production began in January 1874 and ended in July 1882. During this time there were only minor changes in the basic design of the ammunition.

Once removed from their marked cardboard boxes, cartridges for the carbine and rifle were easily confused. This led the Frankford Arsenal to stamp the heads of carbine cartridges "U.S. Carbine." This was done only from March to July 1874. Why the practice was discontinued is unknown. Cartridges produced after July were again indistinguishable. In March 1877 headstamping became a standard practice. An "R" was used to designate the rifle cartridge and a "C" identified the carbine cartridge. Thus C F 5 77 identified a cartridge produced at Frankford Arsenal in the 5th month of 1877.

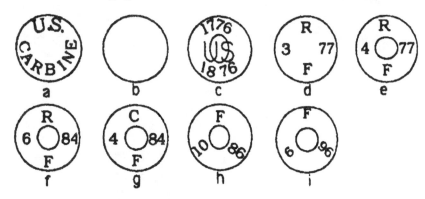

Frankford Arsenal Headstamps
a. U.S. Carbine   b. No headstamp   c. Centennial   d. Early dated   e. Berdan-primed dated   f, g, & h. Middle dated   i. Late dated

At the same time that the Frankford Arsenal was producing cartridges, contract ammunition was also produced by Union Metallic Cartridge Co. at Bridgeport, CT., the United States Cartridge Co. at Lowell, MA., and the Winchester Repeating Arms Co. at New Haven, CT. The UMC cartridges had Berdan priming and brass cases with reinforced heads and were usually headstamped B45-55 (Bridgeport Carbine). U.S Cartridge ammunition usually had Farrington primers, copper-alloy cases (in some instances with a copper gas seal on the face of the rim) and were headstamped RL (Rifle Lowell) with a date. These latter cartridges are rarely found on western military sites.

The balance sheet of the National Armory for June 30, 1878, showed that the cost of the 13,004 carbines and rifles produced in the previous fiscal year was $14.18 per arm. The cost included parts and materials bought during the Civil War which were used in manufacturing carbines, so the actual money outlay was between $10.00 and $11.00 per weapon. As for the actual number of carbines, as of October 1, 1876, there were 6,685 carbines on hand in the army.

The Model 1873 carbine with .45-55-405 ammunition was the shoulder arm of the 7th Cavalry on the Black Hills expedition in 1874. The regiment was delayed in its departure from camp near Fort Abraham Lincoln, Dakota Territory, until the new Springfields arrived on June 29, 1874. By September that year all cavalry regiments had been armed with the Model 1873 carbine, which was to figure prominently in the fight on the Little Bighorn River, Montana Territory, on June 25-26, 1876, when Lieut. Col. George A. Custer attacked a huge village of Sioux and Cheyenne. Major Marcus Reno, who was in the fight (and had been on the 1872 Board which selected the carbine), wrote this letter regarding the faults of the carbine:

Head Qrs 7th Cavalry
Camp on Yellowstone
July 11, 1876

Genl. S. V. Benet
Chf. Ord. U. S. A.

I have the honor to report that in the engagement of the 25 & 26 of June 1876 between the 7th Cav'y & the hostile Sioux that out of 380 carbines in my command six were rendered unserviceable in the following manner, (there were more rendered unserviceable by being struck with bullets) failure of the breechblock to close, leaving a space between the head of the cartridge & the end of the block, & when the piece was discharged, & the block thrown open, the head of the cartridge was pulled off & the cylinder remained in the chamber, whence with the means at hand it was impossible to extract it. I believe this a radical defect, & in the hands of hastily organized troops, would lead to the most disastrous results. The effect results in my opinion in two ways — in the manufacture of the gun the breech block is in many instances so made that it does not fit snug up to the head of the cartridge, after the cartridge is sent home, & it has always been a question in my mind whether the manner in which it revolves into its place does not render a close contact almost impossible to be made — another reason is that the dust, always an element to be considered in the battlefield, prevents the proper closing of the breechblock, & the same result is produced — There may be a want of uniformity in the flange of the head of the cartridge, which would also render the action of the extractor null, in case it was too small, although when the shell was left in the chamber, the head would not be torn off. I also observed another bad fault of the system although it did not render the guns unserviceable — viz. the weight of the breechblock is such that the hinge on which it revolves is very soon loosened, giving to the block a lateral motion, that prevents its closing —

I can also state that the blowing up of the breech block was a contingency that was patent to members of the Board which adopted the system & induced strong opposition to it on the part of a minority. I send you these observations made during a most terrific battle & under circumstances which would induce men to fire with recklessness, as our capture was certain death & torture, & the men fully appreciated the result of falling into the hand of the Indians, & were not as cool perhaps as they would have been fighting a civilized foe. An Indian scout who was with that portion of the Regt. which Custer took into battle, in relating what he saw in that part of the battle, says that from his hiding place he could see the men sitting down under fire & working at their guns — a story that finds confirmation in the fact that officers who afterwards examined the battlefield, as they were burying the dead, found knives with broken blades, lying near the dead bodies. . . . .

Very Resp'y
M. A. Reno

Amt. Ammunition exp'd — Carbine: 38,030   *Maj. 7th Cav'y*
Amt. Ammunition exp'd — Pistol: 2,954   *Comd'g Regt*

First Sergeant William Heyn of Company A, 7th Cavalry, remembered that during the fight, his carbine extractor failed and he had to use a ramrod to push out the empty cases. Lieut. Edward Godfrey of Company K attributed the defeat in part to the defective extraction of the empty cases from the carbine.

Since the action and chambering of both the carbine and rifle were the same and the rifle cartridge (with its larger load) would be more effective over longer distances, the rifle cartridge seemed to be the desired issue for both the rifle and carbine, particularly on the western frontier. Officers and troopers often preferred to fire the .45-70 rifle cartridge in their carbines for the greater range. This preference is recorded in a letter written shortly after the Little Bighorn River fight:

"Office of Chief Ordnance Officer
Chicago, Ill., July 28, 1876

Sir:

My reason for asking for so little carbine ammunition, in comparison with rifle ammunition for the Department of Dakota, is that it is the general impression in the Army that the latter is superior to the former for both arms. The trajectory of the carbine cartridge ball is too much curved, and the range not long enough to cope with the rifle in the hands of Indians. Old huntsmen on the plains tell me they invariably use the 70 grain cartridge with the carbine, and find the recoil not too much.

Within short ranges the carbine shoots too high, while its extreme range is insufficient. I respectfully recommend for your consideration the propriety of using the same cartridge (70 grains powder) in both arms. This would require a corresponding alteration in the rear sight of the carbine.

When our rifles fall into the hands of rifle clubs and huntsmen, the powder charge is invariably increased in the cartridge to 80 or 85 grains.

The complaint against the feebleness of the carbine cartridge is almost universal.

      Very respectfully, your obedient servant
      J. W. Reilly
      Captain of Ordnance" [1]

---

[1] Capt. J. W. Reilly to Chief of Ordnance, Brig. Gen. Stephen Benet, July 20, 1876, Office of Chief of Ordnance, Records Group 156, File 3941, 1876, National Archives.

Although Capt. Reilly indicated preference for the .45-70 cartridge, only about 13 out of 47 unfired cartridges found on the Reno-Benteen battlefield in later years were .45-70s, based on x-rays of the cartridges. However, even some of these are disputed as being .45-70s. One of these is shown here, courtesy of the Midwest Archaeological Center of the Department of the Interior. The remaining 34 were definitely .45-55s. Additional evidence for the presence of .45-70s is as follows:

First Sergeant John Ryan related that before going on the campaign he traded .45-55 cartridges for .45-70 ammunition with First Sergeant William Bolton, Company G, 17th Infantry, for use in his Sharps rifle which he used in the fight.

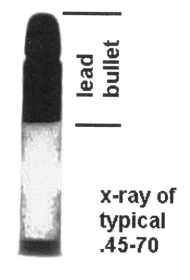

x-ray of typical .45-70

Also, Lieut. Charles Varnum wrote in a letter later that year that he thought the regiment was using the 70-grain cartridge and not the 55-grain ammunition.[2] Certainly .45-70 ammunition was available on the expedition for the 6th and 17th Infantry who were equipped with the Model 1873 rifle, which used the .45-70 cartridge.

W. A. Graham, The Custer Myth - A Source Book of Custeriana (Lincoln, Nebraska: University of Nebraska Press, 1953), page 347.

Lt. Edward Godfrey confirmed that .45-55s and .45-70s were present in the battle during his testimony at Reno's 1879 Court of Inquiry. Godfrey replied to the following questions from Recorder-Lieutenant Jesse Lee:[3]

> Lee: *"Describe what you saw about the condition of the bodies and the evidence of a struggle."*
>
> Godfrey: *". . . .I found a good many cartridge shells but no cartridges that I remember. . . ."*
>
> Lee: *"What were those cartridge shells?"*
>
> Godfrey: *"Carbine shells, caliber .45."*
>
> Lee: *"The same as the troops used or different?"*
>
> Godfrey: **"The same as some of the troops used."** (Emphasis added).

---

[3] Ronald H. Nichols, ed., *Reno Court of Inquiry in the case of Major Marcus A. Reno* (Hardin, Montana: Custer Battlefield Historical and Museum Association, 1995), page 494.

Based on the preceding, it is likely that *both* .45-55 and .45-70 ammunition were used in the Battle of the Little Bighorn. None had headstamps.

As a result of the heated controversy about the merits of the carbine after the Little Bighorn River fight, considerable pressure was exerted to effect changes. As early as 1874 the London <u>Army and Navy Gazette</u> had remarked that *". . . the manufacture of the weapon in both lock and back sight leaves much to be desired."*

During the Indian Wars considerable controversy arose as to the merits of Oliver Winchester's rifles and carbines as compared to the army shoulder arms. This led to a series of tests to determine the relative characteristics of the arms. As shown in Table I, the Model 1873 carbine was clearly a superior weapon to the Winchester Rifle, Model 1873, except that the rifle was a repeating arm.

After 1873 the carbine underwent the changes tabulated in Table II. Changes were progressive from year to year. As weapons came in for repair they were modified by ordnance shops until an issue arm had different dates on the barrel, breech block and receiver, and had early or late model sights, A Special Order dated May 6, 1881, from the Department of Dakota gives an idea of how these changes were made:

> *"Commanding officers of troops of cavalry who desire to have the windguage of the Buck-horn sight for carbines adjusted so as to prevent the lateral motion by sliding are authorized to remove the leaves and mail them to the Fort A. Lincoln Ordnance Depot where they will be adjusted and returned to them . . . ."*

The surviving Model 1873 carbines will often be found to have later changes

Table II provides a check to authenticate, to some degree, individual carbines that have allegedly been used in a frontier fight, by comparing the changes existing in the carbine with the changes listed in Table II up to the date of the fight.

In 1878 a Board On Magazine Guns was convened to consider small-arms changes for the army. The Board recommended continuation of the Springfield carbine but sufficient changes had accrued to warrant production of a new model. The new U. S. Carbine, Model 1877 had a trapdoor in the buttplate to carry the headless shell extractor and jointed cleaning rod that had been advocated as early as 1876. The stacking swivel was omitted — a plain band was substituted. The rear buckhorn sight appeared in four slightly different forms. These sights were introduced by Col. James Benton at the National Armory and were issued from there beginning in 1879. Other minor changes included improved and strengthened lugs and pins; the breech block was stamped "Model 1877" and the weight increased to 7.7 pounds. A total of 19,881 Model 1877 carbines were produced.

By 1882 the army's desire to combine the carbine and rifle into one arm resulted in the U. S. Experimental Carbine, Model 1882. There were three versions with variations in dimensions. One version had a barrel length of 27.75 inches and a stock length of 43.50 inches. The stock length in the second version was 44.25 inches and in the third version the barrel length was 24.75 inches with a stock length of 39.75 inches and an overall length of 43.188 inches. Other descriptions conformed to the regular service carbine, except that the sling swivels were bent to conform to the round of the stock so the carbine could be quickly jerked out of the saddle boot. The experimental carbine was not accepted by troops in the field.

An exterior-primed, copper-cased cartridge was first made in 1879 and became standard in 1882 for the carbine and rifle. In July 1882, production of inside-primed cartridges ended. Manufacture of carbine and rifle cartridges with external Boxer primers began in August. The case was then made with a solid head rather than the folded head of all previous standard types. The charge remained at 55 grains for the carbine and 70 grains for the rifle. The carbine bullet continued at 405 grains while the rifle bullet was increased to 500 grains. In 1886 the over-powder wad was deleted in loading the carbine cartridge and the bullet was seated deeper to take up the extra space.

The army became more interested in reloading cartridges to allow for more range practice and to reduce production costs. The stringent economies that existed in the army during this time are indicated by this curious order from the Chief of Ordnance August 9, 1883:

"Existing orders allow to the cavalry in original cartridges 400 rounds carbine ammunition and 400 rounds revolver ammunition per man, annually, to such troops as are not supplied reloading tools for both

kinds of ammunitions. As reloading tools have been supplied the cavalry for carbine ammunition it is recommended that the allowance be reduced to 240 rounds per man in original cartridges — money value $7.20. Approximately the same as for the infantry with a cost of powder and lead for reloading slightly in favor of the cavalry. That until the cavalry is supplied with reloading tools for revolver ammunition the allowance remains as now, in original cartridges, 400 rounds per man annually. When the tools are supplied that the allowance be reduced to 240 rounds per man annually, original cartridges, money value $4.80. This will allow about an equal number of rounds for the rifle and carbine."

Development continued and in the next model, the U.S. Carbine, Model 1884, the weight increased to 7.9 pounds. The Model 1879 sights were found unsatisfactory and were replaced by the excellent, long-range, flat-leaf sights designed by Col. Adelbert Buffington in the Ordnance Department. The Buffington sight, the first sight capable of windage and elevation adjustment and drift correction, was used on all carbines produced after 1885. Minor changes corresponded to changes made in the U.S. Rifle, Model 1884. The breech block was stamped "Model 1884." Sixty-one of these carbines were issued to Troop M, 7th Cavalry, at Fort Meade, Dakota Territory, in August 1886, for field trial. A total of 20,000 of the Model 1884 carbines were produced through 1889.

The copper-alloy case continued as a source of trouble. It did not contract after firing and thus would stick in the chamber under sustained rapid fire conditions. The case was too soft to allow the extractor to withdraw a jammed cartridge without cutting through the rim or severing the head entirely. The discovery that brass expands quickly when heated and almost as quickly contracts, put an eventual end to federal production of copper cases. The Frankford Arsenal began production of brass-cased cartridges in July 1888, and continued production until June 1898, though manufacture for the regular army ceased in 1895. Most brass cases from Frankford Arsenal were tinned inside and out to protect against deterioration due to mercuric priming and corrosion. As usual, cartridges were also obtained on federal contract from commercial sources. Contract cartridges had brass cases and, in many instances, the manufacturer's usual commercial headstamp.

An experimental cavalry carbine with a 24-inch barrel was introduced in 1886 in an attempt to equip troops with a more effective shoulder weapon. One thousand were produced but development was stopped by 1891 because of the increasing interest in the development of a smokeless-powder, magazine weapon.

When the carbine link was replaced by a saddle boot, damage to the rear sight and loss of the front sight cover sometimes resulted. This was corrected by the manufacture of a new rear sight guard and a secured front cover for installation at ordnance depots. A modified front sight cover was added and secured by a pin and the barrel band was modified by a humpback, sloping projection to protect the rear sight in rough handling or when thrust into the saddle boot. Between July, 1873, and June, 1889, a total of 59,909 carbines were produced at the National Armory. Manufacture of the Springfield carbine was discontinued in June 1889. This was the last of the .45-55 carbines, the last to use black powder, the last of the large calibers and the last single-shot carbine to be used by the army. The carbine had seen service in every conceivable weather condition from the sub-zero cold of the Dakota prairies to the heat of the Sonoran desert. The cavalry used the carbine in many of the almost one thousand Indian fights by the army.

Many states received replacements for their antiquated militia arms from the stocks of carbines in storage. National Guard units used the Springfield carbine as late as 1906. The Model 1884 was the usual volunteer arm in the Spanish-American War, though the regular army by that time had been armed with the Krag-Jorgenson bolt-action carbine. The Springfield was considered unsatisfactory as the smoke from the black powder gave away the troop position to the enemy but Brig. Gen. Frederick Funston said of the Springfield, *"If a bullet from one of them hit a man, he never mistook it for a mosquito bite."*

The replacement weapon, the Model 1899 Krag-Jorgenson carbine issued from 1899 to 1902, used the .30/40 Krag smokeless centerfire cartridge manufactured at the Frankford Arsenal. Soldiers complained that the Krag did not have the stopping power of the Springfield.

As early as 1883 the firm of Hartley & Graham of 17-19 Maiden Lane, New York City, had sold surplus stocks of the U. S. Carbine, Model 1873, to dealers. After replacement by the Krag, large quantities of the Springfield carbines were placed on the market and became favorite big-game guns in the west. In 1916 the War Department offered 32,000 serviceable Springfield carbines and rifles for sale at 75 cents each. Carbine ammunition was offered at $12 per 1,000 rounds.

Thus ended the active use of the Springfield carbines in the army and the commencement of a new era, that of acquiring the carbine for sporting purposes or specialty collections. Today Springfield carbines command premium prices and are treasured by their owners. As a measure of their popularity the Navy Arms Co. of Ridge-field, N.J. has imported an excellent working replica of the 1873 carbine using the .45-70-405 cartridge. The gun is manufactured by Davide Pedersoli in Brescia, Italy.

TABLE I COMPARISON OF SPRINGFIELD CARBINE AND WINCHESTER RIFLE

MEAN VELOCITIES

Springfield with 10 rifle cartridges . . . . 1363.5 ft./sec.
Springfield with 10 carbine cartridges. . . . . . 1166.6 ft./sec.
Winchester with 8 Winchester cartridges . . . 1127.4 ft/sec.

MEAN DEVIATION (inches)	100	200	500	900 yards
Springfield with rifle cartridge	3.17	8.36	14.03	35.12
Springfield with carbine cartridge	2.48	7.97	19.05	36.52
Winchester	2.27	12.27	21.56	Not obtainable

PENETRATION IN WHITE PINE AT 100 YARDS

	Mean of 5 Shots (inches)	Bullet Weight (grains)	Powder Weight (grains)
Springfield	10.075	405	55
Spencer, .50 cal.	6.95	348	59½
Spencer, .50 cal.	8.25	430	55
Winchester	4.9	200	40

These comparison tests were made by Lieut. John C. Greer at the Springfield Armory, August 11, 1876. The Springfield weapon used was the U. S. Carbine, Model 1873, .45 Caliber. The Winchester Rifle, Model 1873, was tested. This rifle weighed 8.6 pounds empty and 9.27 pounds with 15 cartridges.

TABLE II — ORDNANCE CHANGES IN THE SPRINGFIELD CARBINE

Mar. 1876	Instead of being notched, the underside of the firing pin guard was cut away to the end of the guard.
Jan. 1877	The 1877 rear sight differed from the previous models in position and number of graduation marks, shape of sighting notch and other changes. There were offsets on the base of the first form of Model 1877 sight.
Mar. 1878	The arch of the breech block was filled to increase block strength and the breech block and breech block screw were case-hardened in water.
Apr. 1878	The breech block hinge pin was broached instead of reamed.
May 1878	The second form of Model 1877 sight had a continuous curve of base.
June 1878	Firing pin spring omitted. Shoulder for firing pin spring omitted and that portion of the pin was made conical.

Oct. 1878   The breech block height of comb and the breech block width were increased and the angle at front and rear ends of flanges were rounded. Thickness of metal increased on top, front end of receiver. Breech block hinge pin was lengthened to correspond with altered receiver. Receiver width increased the whole length. Extractor lug was increased slightly in height. Rear end of barrel tenon rounded to fit bottom of counterbore in front end of receiver. All reentrant angles and bottom of counterbore for barrel tenon were rounded. Rear end of barrel groove in stock slightly widened and deepened to receive enlarged receiver. Gas escape ports made deeper and extended to rear.

Jan. 1879   The Model 1879 rear sight differed from previous models in having a buckhorn shaped eyepiece (instead of the old V shape notched eyepiece) attached to side when moved laterally to correct for wind and drift and errors in construction of piece. There was no lateral motion at 100 yd. elevation where sight notch was intended to be over axis of arm. First of four forms of Model 1879 sight had windage graduation marks .02" apart with projecting points on lower edge of buckhorn plate. Slotted heads cut into base screws for screwdriver use.

Apr. 1879   Case-hardening of breech block cap omitted and cap blackened after fitting. Firing pin was tempered.

Oct. 1879   Second form of 1879 sight had windage graduation marks .04" apart. Projecting points on lower edge of buckhorn plate were cut off. Centering pin in buckhorn plate made in wide V shape. Upper edge of buckhorn plate made straight with large semi-circular notch.

Nov. 1879   Third form of 1879 sight had upper surface of leaf hinge flattened.

Dec. 1879   Band with stacking swivel omitted and lower band of rifle substituted.

Jan. 1880   Lip cut under side of head of hammer. Rear end of hardened carbine front sight made nearly vertical instead of beveled.

Apr. 1880   Main spring swivel rivet tempered instead of being left soft.

July 1880   Fourth form of 1879 sight had semi-circular notch on lower edge of buckhorn plate for centering pin. Large notch between buckhorns made straight at bottom instead of rounded and beveled toward front.

Jan. 1881   Firing pin slot rounded at corners.

Aug. 1881   Butt plate made heavier and form changed to provide trapdoor.

Jan. 1883   Thumb piece cut away to prevent striking lock plate.

Mar. 1883   Straight corrugated trigger adopted.

Oct. 1883   Detachable front sight cover issued.

Jan. 1885   Sear nose widened. Notches of tumbler widened to correspond with wide sear.

Sept. 1885 Front sights of new model carbines made thinner at base. Front sight height raised to .738" above axis of bore. Rear edge of sight made vertical. Top of front sight slightly rounded and polished to provide bead.
Mar. 1886 Front sight cover made component part of carbine.
June 1886 Camlatch and thumbpiece riveted with end of shaft not ground off to remove riveting marks. Top surface of band transversely grooved to accommodate Model 1884 rear sight.
Aug. 1886 Angle of sear notch changed to prevent sear nose catching on safety notch. 1884 rear sight modified after issue of enlarging windage and binding screw heads to provide more grip to fingers and to overlap sides of leaf when down to give more lateral leaf support. Action of binding screw on side changed to hold it firm. Movable base and slide were case-hardened.
Dec. 1886 Firing pin to be made of aluminum-bronze thereafter when available.
Feb. 1888 New model front sight cover approved.
Nov. 1889 Front sight made to same thickness above stud as that of rifle.
Feb. 1890 Trigger guard strap and bow made in one piece and in different shape.
Oct. 1890 Rear sight protector band approved.
Dec. 1890 Front sight cover modified and secured by pin. Front sight height lowered to .728" above axis of bore.

TABLE III STANDARD SERVICE CARTRIDGES MANUFACTURED AT FRANKFORD ARSENAL 1866-1898

Date	Cal.	Pdr Wt. (gr)	Bullet Wt. (gr)	Priming	Case
Oct. 66 - Mar. 68	.50	70	450	Inside, Center Fire, Martin bar anvil	Copper, straight, 1.75"
Mar. 68 - Sept. 69	.50	70	450	Inside, CF, Benet tinned iron cup	Copper, straight, 1.75"
Sept. 69 - Aug.70	.50	70	450	Inside, CF, Benet tinned iron cup	Same with cylindrical throat
Aug. 70 - Nov. 71	.50	70	450	Inside, CF, Benet deep copper cup	Copper, straight, 1.75"
Dec. 71- Dec. 73	.50	70	450	Inside, CF, Benet shallow copper cup	Copper, straight, 1.75"
May 71- Oct. 71	.50	70	450	Inside, CF, Martin pocket, short bar anvil	Copper, straight, 1.75"
Nov. 71 - Dec. 71	.50	70	450	Inside, CF, Martin pocket, disk anvil	Copper, straight, 1.75"

Date	Cal.	Powder	Bullet	Primer	Case
Jan. 72 - Dec. 73	.50	55	450	Inside, CF, Benet shallow copper cup	Copper, straight, 1.319"
Sept. 73 - July 82	.45	55	405	Inside, CF, Benet cup	Copper, straight, 2.10"
Jan. 74 - July 82	.45	70	405	Inside, CF, Benet cup	Copper, straight, 2.10"
July 82 - June 88	.45	55	405	External primer Boxer	Copper, straight, 2.10" solid head
July 82 - June 88	.45	70	500	External primer Boxer	Copper, straight, 2.10" solid head
July 88 - 1898	.45	55	405	Boxer	Tinned brass, straight solid head, 2.10"
July 88 - 1898	.45	70	500	Boxer	Tinned brass, straight solid head, 2.10"
1880 - 1884	.45	80	500	Boxer	Copper, straight, 2.40" solid head
1886 - 1888	.45	70	500	Boxer	Tinned brass, straight, 2.10" Morse reloading cartridge

TABLE IV   PRODUCTION OF SPRINGFIELD CARBINES

CALENDAR YEAR	QUANTITY	NOTES
1869	3	
1871	361a	a. 313 Model 1870 carbines were made and issued for field trials.
1873	1,942	
1874	10,873	
1875	7,211	
1876	2b	b. Includes one with Metcalfe cartridge-holding attachment.
1877	2,496	
1878	2,000c	c. Model 1877
1880	14,884	
1881	501	
1886	6,000d	d. 5000 Model 1884 carbines and 1000 carbines with 24" barrels.
1887	5,000e	e. Model 1884
1888	5,000f	f. Includes one carbine with 24" barrel
1889	5,000g	g. Includes two carbines with 24" barrels

Charles Hanson, "Springfield Shoulder Arms," The American Rifleman, Jan.1965, 113:1 (71-72); Malden Waite and Bernard Ernst, Trapdoor Springfield: The United States Single Shot Rifle 1865-1893, 1980, North Hollywood: Beinfeld.

TABLE V — SERIAL NUMBERS OF SPRINGFIELD CARBINES

Year of Manufacture	Quarter	Number of Carbines	Number of Other Arms	Serial Numbers
1873	Jul - Sep	2	2	1 - 4
	Oct - Dec	1,940	2	5 - 1,946
1874	Jan - Mar	2,124	6,522	1,947 - 10,592
	Apr - Jun	5,956	11,484	10,593 - 28,032
	Jul - Sep	31	1,655	28,033 - 29,718
	Oct - Dec	2,762	2,738	29,719 - 35,218
1875	Jan - Mar	7,211	2,610	35,219 - 45,039
	Apr - Dec	0	15,286	45,040 - 60,325
1876	Jan - Mar	1	3,838	60,326 - 64,164
	Apr - Sep	0	5,982	64,165 - 71,673
	Oct - Dec	1	2,539	71,674 - 74,213
1877	Jan - Mar	2	16	74,214 - 74,231
	Apr - Jun	2,494	0	74,232 - 76,725
	Jul - Dec	0	0	
1878	Jan - Mar	0	4,501	76,726 - 81,226
	Apr - Jun	2,000	6,503	81,227 - 89,729
	Jul - Dec	0	10,666	89,730 - 100,395
1879	Jan - Dec	0	19,778	100,396 - 119,273
1880	Jan - Mar	4,382	2,298	119,274 - 125,953
	Apr - Jun	1,003	3,184	125,954 - 130,140
	Jul - Sep	2,241	4,164	130,141 - 136,545
	Oct - Dec	7,258	716	136,546 - 144,519
1881	Jan - Mar	0	7,703	144,520 - 151,222
	Apr - Jun	501	4,977	151,223 - 156,700
	Jul - Dec	0	8,196	156,701 - 164,896
1882	Jan - Dec	0	28,919	164,897 - 193,815
1883	Jan - Dec	0	34,756	193,816 - 228,571
1884	Jan - Dec	0	35,305	228,572 - 263,876
1885	Jan - Dec	0	42,178	263,877 - 306,054

1886	Jan - Mar	0	9,803	306,055 - 315,857
	Apr - Jun	5,000	1,000	315,858 - 326,773
	Jul - Dec	0	20,002	326,774 - 346,775
1887	Jan - Mar	200	9,702	346,776 - 356,677
	Apr - Jun	4,800	6,402	356,678 - 367,879
	Jul - Dec	0	19,766	367,880 - 387,645
1888	Jan - Mar	3,361	7,201	387,646 - 398,207
	Apr - Jun	1,639	9,063	398,208 - 408,909
	Jul - Dec	0	19,860	408,910 - 428,769
1889	Jan - Mar	2,920	7,747	428,770 - 439,436
	Apr - Jun	2,080	8,765	439,437 - 450,281

TABLE VI   RANGE OF SERIAL NUMBERS OF CARBINES USED IN THE BATTLE OF THE LITTLE BIGHORN

The following serial numbers were from carbines taken from the Indians in the months following battle:

Number of carbines	Serial numbers			
3	1,196	3,146	3,197	
8	17,485	17,940	18,137	18,141
	18,202	20,498	21,573	21,669
6	33,155	33,815	34,723	36,442
	39,253	42,259		

<u>Source:</u> Report of the Chief of Ordnance, Ordnance Note #CXV, October 1, 1879.

Based on the above and other evidence, the Springfield Record Service of Silver Springs, MD, reports carbines used in the battle must be in the following ranges. Of course, not all carbines in these ranges were used in the battle. About 585 carbines were present for the enlisted men. There were an unknown additional number for the officers, quartermaster employees, civilians and scouts, but likely did not exceed 670 total.

    1,000 - 3,197
    12,200 - 28,032
    31,000 - 43,600

BIBLIOGRAPHY

Annual Reports of the Chief of Ordnance to the Secretary of War, 1873 Through 1890, Washington, DC: Government Printing Office (GPO).
Arnold, Ralph, "U.S. Cavalry Carbine Slings," Gun Report, February, 1974, 19:9, Aledo, IL.
Barber, John, *The Rimfire Cartridge In The United States And Canada: An Illustrated History Of Its Manufacture And The Products, 1857 To 1984*, (Tacoma, WA: Armory Publications, 1987).
Barnes, Frank, *Cartridges Of The World* (Chicago, IL: Follett Publishing Co.,1969).
Butler, David, *United States Firearms: The First Century, 1776-1875* (New York, NY: Winchester Press, 1971).
Campbell, H.S., "The Finest .45-70 Ever Built," American Rifleman, November, 1933.
Chapell, Charles, *Guns Of The Old West* (New York, NY: Coward-McCann, Inc., 1961).
Catalog Of The Arms And Accoutrements Of The National Armory (Springfield, MA: Springfield National Armory, July 1, 1909).
Datig, Fred, *Cartridges For Collectors* (Los Angeles, CA: Borden Publishing Co., 1956, 1958, 1967), Volumes I-III.
Description And Rules For The Management Of The Springfield Rifle, Carbine And Army Revolvers, Caliber .45, 1874, 1876, 1878, 1882, 1886, 1890, 1891, 1898, Washington, DC: GPO.
Descriptive Catalog Of The Ordnance Museum, Rock Island Arsenal, 1909, Rock Island, IL: Rock Island Arsenal.
Du Mont, John and John Parsons, *Firearms In The Custer Battle* (Harrisburg, PA: The Stackpole Co., 1953).
Du Mont, John, *Custer Battle Guns* (Fort Collins, CO: Old Army Press, 1974).
Executive Document No.16, "The Cost Of Manufactures At The National Armory Springfield Massachusetts January 7, 1879," Washington, DC: GPO.
Frasca, Albert and Robert Hill, *The .45-70 Springfield* (Northridge, CA: Springfield Publishing Co., 1980).
Frasca, Albert, *The .45-70 Springfield, Book II, Springfield Calibers .58, .50, .45 and .30 Breech Loaders In The U.S. Service 1865-1893* (Springfield, OH: Frasca Publishing Co., 1997).
Frasca, Albert, The Trapdoor Springfield Newsletter, Volumes 1-3, 1998-99, Springfield, OH: Frasca Publishing Co.
Fuller, Claude, *The Breech-loader In Service - A History Of All Standard And Experimental Breech-loading And Magazine Shoulder Arms* (New Milford, CT: Norm Flayderman, 1965).

Garavaglia, Louis and Charles Worman, "Search For A Breech-loading Carbine," American Rifleman, August, 1977.

Garavaglia, Louis and Charles Worman, *Firearms Of The American West, 1866-1894* (College Station, TX: Creative Publishing Co., 1986).

Gluckman, Arcadi, *United States Muskets, Rifles And Carbines* (Buffalo, NY: Otto Ulbrich Co., 1948).

Hackley, F. W., et al, *History Of Modern U. S. Military Small Arms Ammunition* (New York, NY: Macmillan Co., 1967).

Hacker, Rick, ".45-70 - Getting Older, Getting Better," American Rifleman, May, 1979.

Harrison, E. H., "Reviving Ghosts," American Rifleman, August, 1931.

Hardin, Albert and Robert Hedden, *Light But Efficient* (Dallas, TX: Taylor Publishing Co., 1973).

Hedren, Paul, "Carbine Extraction Failure At The Little Bighorn: A New Examination," Military Collector And Historian, 1973, 25:2, 66-68.

Herr, John and Edgar Wallace, *The Story of the U.S. Cavalry 1775-1942* (New York: Bonanza Books, 1981).

Hicks, James, *U. S. Military Firearms, 1776 - 1956* (LaCanada, CA: J. E. Hicks & Sons, 1962).

Hicks, James, Notes On United States Ordnance, Volume 1, Small Arms, 1776 to 1946, 1946, Mt. Vernon, NY: private printing.

Hoyem, George, *Historical Development Of Small Arms Ammunition* (Tacoma, WA: Armory Publications, 1981).

Jackson, Archer, "Rare Trapdoor Springfields," Bulletin Of American Society of Arms Collectors, Fall 1967, Spring 1968, Nos.16 and 17.

Jenkins, P. B. "The Finest .45-70 Springfield Ever Built," American Rifleman, September, 1929.

Keith, Elmer, "The Officer's Model 1873 Springfield," American Rifleman, October, 1936.

Kronfeld, John "Loading The .45-70 For Classic Rifles," American Rifleman, July, 1998.

Lewis, Berkley, *Small Arms Ammunition At The International Exposition Philadelphia, 1876* (Washington, DC: Smithsonian Institution Press, 1972).

Lewis, Berkley, "Small Arms Ammunition In The United States Service, 1776-1865," Smithsonian Miscellaneous Collections, Volume 129, August 14, 1946, Washington, DC: Smithsonian Institution Press.

Linden, Alvin, "Dressing Up The .45-70 Springfield," American Rifleman, July, 1936.

Logan, Herschel, *Cartridges, A Pictorial Digest Of Small Arms Ammunition* (Huntington, CA: Standard Publications, 1948; New York, NY: Bonanza Books, 1959; and Harrisburg, PA: The Stackpole Co., 1959).

Losey, Timothy, "Missing Guns Of The 7th Cavalry," <u>Men At Arms</u>, 1995, No.4.

Marcot, Roy, *Hiram Berdan, Military Commander And Firearms Inventor* (Irvine, CA: Northwood Heritage Press).

McChristian, Douglas, *An Army Of Marksmen* (Fort Collins, CO: Old Army Press, 1981).

Meketa, Ray, *Model 1873 Springfield Carbine* (Douglas, AK: Cheechako Press, 1984). Self published, 100 copies.

Michno, Greg, "Guns Of The Little Bighorn," <u>Wild West</u>, June, 1998, 11:1, Dorrance Publishing Co.

<u>The National Armory, Weekly and Quarterly Report of Arms Manufactured Repaired, Issued And Ready For Issue, 1874 to 1890</u>, Springfield, MA: Springfield National Armory.

Noyes, Lee, "A Question of Arms: Ordnance Causes and Consequences of the Little Bighorn," <u>11th Annual Symposium, Custer Battlefield Historical & Museum Association Held at Hardin, Montana on June 27, 1997</u>.

<u>Ordnance Memoranda No.14</u>, "Metallic Cartridges (Regular and Experimental) As Manufactured And Tested At The Frankford Arsenal, Philadelphia, PA, 1873," Washington, DC: GPO, T. J. Treadwell.

<u>Ordnance Memoranda No.15</u>, "Officers Report, The Proper Caliber For Small Arms," Bureau Of Ordnance, 1873, Washington, DC: GPO.

<u>Ordnance Memoranda No.21</u>, "Ammunition, Fuzes, Primers, Military Pyrotechny," 1878, Washington, DC: GPO. Stephen Benét and James Whittemore.

<u>Ordnance Memoranda No.22</u>, "Fabrication Of Small Arms For The U.S. Service," 1878, Washington, DC: GPO.

<u>Ordnance Memoranda No.43</u>, "War Department Comparison Of Lined With Wad Cartridges," 1875, Washington, DC: GPO.

Pitman, John, *The Pitman Notes On U.S. Martial Small Arms and Ammunition 1776-1933, Volume 3, U.S. Breech-loading Rifles and Carbines, Cal. 45* (Gettysburg, PA: Thomas Publications, 1991).

Poyer, Joe and Craig Riesch, *The .45-70 Springfield* (Tustin, CA: North Cape Publications, 1999, 3rd edition).

Reilly, Robert, *United States Military Small Arms 1816-1865* (Baton Rouge: The Eagle Press, 1970).

Reno, Marcus, "Letter From Major Reno July 11, 1876, to Col. S. V. Benét, Chief Of Ordnance, regarding the Springfield Carbine in the Little Bighorn River Fight," The Army and Navy Journal, August 19, 1876, Volume 14, p.26. The original letter is in the Office Of The Chief of Ordnance, National Archives & Records Administration, Washington, DC.

Report Of The Secretary Of War, Ordnance, Volume III, 1885, Washington, DC: GPO.

Reuland, Walter, *Cartridges For The Springfield Trapdoor Rifles And Carbines, 1865-1898* (Laramie, WY: Heritage Concepts, 1991).

Sharpe, Philip, *The Rifle In America* (New York: Funk & Wagnalls Co., 1947, 2nd edition).

Shields, Joseph, *From Flintlock to M-1* (New York, NY: Coward-McCann, Inc., 1954.).

Shockley, Philip, *The Trapdoor Springfield In The Service* (Aledo, IL: World Wide Gun Report, Inc., 1958, 9th edition).

"Small Arms Ammunition At The International Exposition," 1972, Smithsonian Studies In History and Technology, Washington, DC: Smithsonian Institution.

Suydam, Charles, *U. S. Cartridges And Their Handguns, 1795 to 1975* (North Hollywood, CA: Beinfeld Publishing Co., 1977).

Stockbridge, V.D., *Digest Of U.S. Patents Relating To Breech-loading And Magazine Small Arms 1836-1873* (Greenwich, CT: Norm Flayderman, Reprinted 1963).

Sword, Wiley, "7th Cavalry Serial Numbers Springfield Carbines," *Guns At The Little Bighorn* (Lincoln, RI: Andrew Mowbray, Inc., 1988).

Triggs, James, "Springfield Model 1873 .45-70 Rifle," American Rifleman, June, 1960.

Vagar, J. V. K., "A Cut Down .45-70," Field And Stream, October, 1926.

Vagar, J. V. K., "Single-shot Rifles," American Rifleman, June, 1940.

Waite, Malden, "Single-shot That Wouldn't Surrender: The U.S. .45-70," American Rifleman, August, 1973.

Waite, Malden and Bernard Ernst, *Trapdoor Springfield: The United States Springfield Single Shot Rifle, 1865-1893* (North Hollywood, CA: Beinfeld Publishing Co.1980, first edition; Highland Park, NJ: The Gun Room Press second edition).

Weibert, Don, *Custer, Cases and Cartridges: The Weibert Collection Analyzed* (Billings, MT: Don Weibert, 1989).

Whelen, Townsend, Small Arms Design And Ballistics, Volume II, 1946.

Whelen, Townsend, "The .45-70 Springfield Rifle," American Rifleman, January, 1935.

Comparison data between the Winchester Rifle Model 1873 and the U.S. Carbine Model 1873, was published in The Army and Navy Journal, August 26, 1876, XIV:3, p. 43. The Journal has much material pertaining to the weapons of the army and the issues in the Indian Wars period include articles on the Springfield carbine as well as experimental and field trial weapons.